YOUR RESPIRATION and CIRCULATION

Understand Them with Numbers

Melanie Waldron

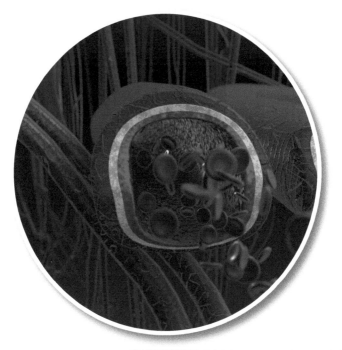

Raintree

Chicago, Illinois

Produced for Raintree by
White-Thomson Publishing
www.wtpub.co.uk
+44 (0)843 208 7460

Edited by Sonya Newland
Designed by Tim Mayer
Original illustrations © Capstone 2014
Illustrated by HL Studios
Picture research by Sonya Newland
Production by Victoria Fitzgerald
Originated by Capstone Global Library Ltd

**Library of Congress Cataloging-in-Publication
Data**
Waldron, Melanie.
  Your respiration and circulation : understand it
with numbers / Melanie Waldron.
    pages cm.—(Your body by numbers)
Includes bibliographical references and index.
  ISBN 978-1-4109-5983-6 (hb)
  ISBN 978-1-4109-5988-1 (pb)
  1. Respiration—Juvenile literature. 2. Lungs—
Juvenile literature. 3. Blood—Circulation—Juve-
nile literature. I. Title.

  QP121.W33 2014
  612.2—dc23   2013016819

Acknowledgments
Corbis p. 29 top (Denis Scott); Dreamstime
pp. 5 (Jonmilnes), 9 top (Akarelias), 11 bottom
(Imagerymajestic), 13 top (Chrispethick),
15 bottom (Kineticimagery), 18 top (Arkadi
Bojaršinov), 19 top (Stefanolunardi), 21
bottom (Steveheap), 22 (Fenton1806), 27 right
(Iakov Filimonov), 31 (Turhanerbas), 33 bottom
(Robert Adrian Hillman), 34 top (Gnanavel
Subramani), 34 bottom (Juri Samsonov), 35
(Sebastian Kaulitzki), 43 (Monkey Business
Images); Shutterstock pp. 4 (Diego Cervo), 6
(Irina Yun), 7 bottom (leungchopan), 11 top
(Amir Ridhwan), 12 (Jose AS Reyes), 16
(bikeriderlondon), 17 (wdeon), 21 top (Sebastian
Kaulitzki), 24 bottom (leungchopan), 25 top
(Africa Studio), 26 (Andi Berger), 28 (Loonello
Calvetti), 29 bottom (chalabala), 30 top (OPIS
Zagreb), 33 top (Emcgiq), 36 right, 40 top
(Donna Beeler), 41 top (BlueRingMedia),
45 (caimacanul); SuperStock pp. 8 (Daghlian/
Phanie), 13 bottom (Science Photo Library),
14 (Hank Grebe/Purestock), 23 top (Tips
Images), 23 bottom (JOSE OTO/BSIP), 24 top
(Science Photo Library), 27 left (Science Picture
Co/Science Faction), 32 (Voisin/Phanie), 37
(Biosphoto), 38 (Corbis), 41 bottom (Phanie).

Cover photograph of the respiratory system
reproduced with permission of Alex Mit/
Shutterstock.

Every effort has been made to contact copyright
holders of any material reproduced in this book.
Any omissions will be rectified in subsequent
printings if notice is given to the publisher.

CONTENTS

Some words are shown in bold, **like this**. You can find out what they mean by looking in the glossary.

Breathing Life into Your Body

Every minute, every day, your lungs breathe air into your body and your heart beats. Your blood links your lungs and your heart. Your lungs supply life-giving oxygen to your blood, and your heart pushes your blood around all the parts of your body.

When you exercise, your heart beats quickly and you breathe more deeply. This is because your brain is instructing your lungs to take in more air.

Auto-control

You decide about and control most of your body's movements, your thoughts, and your actions. But it is your brain that controls how you breathe and how your heart beats. When you are sleeping, your brain keeps your lungs breathing and your heart beating.

When you are exercising, your brain tells your lungs to take in more air and your heart to pump faster. It does this by sending messages at up to 270 miles (435 kilometers) per hour along **nerve cells** to these **organs**.

A Job for Life

In your whole life, your heart will never take a break. Over a period of 75 years, it will beat around three billion times—sometimes fast, sometimes slow. You can hold your breath for a while, but after that, your brain takes over and makes you start breathing again. You take about 20,000 breaths every day.

Extreme Breath-holding

How long can you hold your breath? Thirty seconds? A minute? The world record is over 22 minutes! This was set by a free diver—someone who dives underwater without breathing equipment. For the world record, he remained motionless in a tank of water for 22 minutes and 22 seconds.

Free divers must train to be able to dive deep underwater without breathing equipment. The current world record is a dive of 702 feet (214 meters) below the surface of the water.

Take a Breath...

Your respiratory system is the part of your body that deals with breathing. It starts with your nose and mouth and ends with tiny little pockets inside your lungs.

What Are You Breathing?

You breathe in air. The important part of air that your body needs is a gas called **oxygen**. Oxygen makes up about 21 percent of the air. The rest is made of nitrogen (about 78 percent) and other gases (about 1 percent), including carbon dioxide.

Your body needs oxygen in its **cells**—the tiny building blocks that make up all the parts of your body. Oxygen helps cells release energy from **glucose** in your blood. The glucose gets into your blood from the food that you eat.

Your body gets energy from the food you eat and the oxygen you breathe.

In Through the Nose...

When you breathe in, tiny hairs inside your nose catch any large particles of dirt and dust in the air. A layer of sticky mucus traps finer particles and some **germs**.

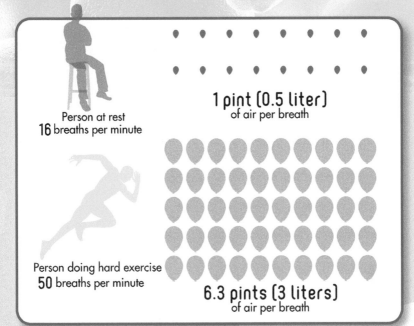

Person at rest
16 breaths per minute

1 pint (0.5 liter)
of air per breath

Person doing hard exercise
50 breaths per minute

6.3 pints (3 liters)
of air per breath

Changing Volumes

When you are sitting quietly at rest, each breath you take is about 1 pint (0.5 liter) of air. You take about 16 breaths every minute. After hard exercise, each breath takes in 5.3–6.3 pints (5–3 liters) of air, and you take about 50 breaths every minute. This increase is because your cells need more oxygen, to convert more glucose, to give them more energy, so you can move more!

This diagram shows the amount of air taken in by a person at rest and a person doing hard exercise.

Snot

All the dust, dirt, and germs that your nose traps mixes with mucus to become… snot! Some of this comes out when you blow (or even pick) your nose. The rest? You swallow about a glassful every day!

Down the Windpipe

Air goes down the back of your nose, past your throat, and into your windpipe (also called the trachea). The windpipe runs next to your esophagus, which carries food down to your stomach. A little flap covers your windpipe when you swallow, so that food does not go down it.

Your windpipe is lined with millions of tiny hairs called cilia. These catch any bits of dust and dirt that get in. They make waving movements that push the mucus upward and away from your lungs.

Your windpipe is surrounded by 16–20 rings of a tough, bendable material called cartilage. This keeps it rigid enough to stay open and allow air to pass through, but bendable enough so that you can move your neck.

Bronchial Tree

At the bottom end of the windpipe, it splits into two branches called **bronchi**. One goes to the left lung and the other goes to the right lung. The bronchi keep splitting into two treelike branches. They divide like this about 15 times, getting smaller each time. Eventually, they become very thin little tubes called **bronchioles**.

Cilia in your lungs push the mucus upward and out. You either cough it up—or swallow it!

Long Neck, Long Trachea

You might expect giraffes to have long windpipes because of their long necks…and you would be right! An adult giraffe's windpipe is about 69 inches (175 centimeters) long.

A giraffe draws air through its windpipe at about 6½ feet (2 meters) per second—about twice as fast as a human breathes in air.

This diagram shows the lengths of some of the different "branches" in the bronchial tree. The smallest branches, the bronchioles, are very short and narrow.

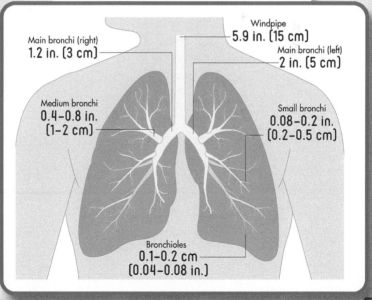

Windpipe
5.9 in. (15 cm)

Main bronchi (right)
1.2 in. (3 cm)

Main bronchi (left)
2 in. (5 cm)

Medium bronchi
0.4–0.8 in.
(1–2 cm)

Small bronchi
0.08–0.2 in.
(0.2–0.5 cm)

Bronchioles
0.1–0.2 cm
(0.04–0.08 in.)

Voice Box

Your **respiratory system** also plays a role in letting you speak!
You make your voice sounds in your voice box (also called the larynx),
at the top of your windpipe. This contains two flaps called vocal
cords. Muscles in the larynx shorten and pull the vocal cords
together, like curtains. Air from your lungs is pushed between the
vocal cords, which vibrate and make the sounds of your voice.

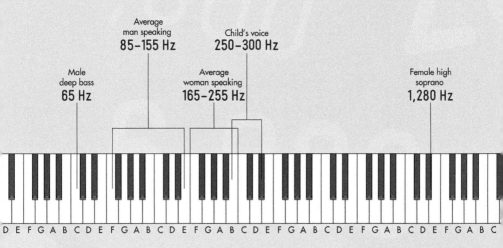

Average
man speaking
85–155 Hz

Child's voice
250–300 Hz

Male
deep bass
65 Hz

Average
woman speaking
165–255 Hz

Female high
soprano
1,280 Hz

D E F G A B C D E F G A B C D E F G A B C D E F G A B C D E F G A B C D E F G A B C D E F G A B C

The pitch of a voice is measured in units
called hertz (Hz). This means the number
of sound waves per second.

What's Your Pitch?

When the vocal cords are pulled loosely together, you make
low-pitched sounds—like the keys toward the left side of a
piano keyboard. When they are pulled tightly together, you
make high-pitched sounds. You use your lips and tongue to
fine-tune these sounds to make words.

Normalhumanspeechis between55–70decibels, but we can speak much more quietly…

…or much louder!

Shouting and Whispering

The volume of a voice can be measured in units called decibels. You change the volume by altering the amount of air that passes over your vocal cords. Whispering needs only a tiny bit of air, but when you shout you need to take a big breath first, so there is more air to push out. Talking only works well with breathed-out air. It sounds odd when you talk while breathing in.

No Need to Shout!

In 1994, a teacher from Northern Ireland broke the world record for the loudest shout. Annalisa Flanagan shouted the word *quiet* and managed to reach a noise level of 121.7 decibels. That's about as loud as a jet engine!

11

Drawing in Oxygen

You breathe in order to pull oxygen into your lungs. But exactly how do you do that? And what happens to the oxygen once it reaches your lungs? Breathing in and out is possible because of the muscles in your ribs, called intercostals, and a large muscle below the lungs, called the diaphragm.

Breathing Muscles

When you breathe in, the diaphragm contracts and flattens out. This pulls your lungs down and makes them bigger. Also, the intercostals pull your ribs outward, making your lungs stretch out. These actions lower the air pressure inside your lungs, and this draws in air from the outside.

When you breathe out, the intercostals and the diaphragm relax. This lets your lungs spring back to their normal smaller size, and so air is pushed out.

At rest, up to 21 pints (10 liters) of air moves in and out of your lungs every minute. This rises to around 425 pints (200 liters) during hard exercise.

You use your breathing muscles, and muscles in your face, to blow up a balloon.

Total Lung Capacity

The total capacity of your lungs is the maximum amount of air you can hold in your lungs. For an adult, the average is 12.3 pints (5.8 liters). A blue whale, the largest animal on Earth, has a lung capacity of 1,320 gallons (5,000 liters)! A horse has a lung capacity of 15 gallons (55 liters).

A little mouse has a total lung capacity of only 0.03 ounce (1 milliliter).

Spongy Lungs

In your lungs, the smallest bronchioles are thinner than a human hair. At the ends are **alveoli**, which are like tiny air bubbles in a sponge. The smallest ones are only about 0.001 inch (0.025 millimeter) in diameter.

Each lung has around 300–400 million alveoli, making a huge surface area inside the lungs. If you spread out all the alveoli, the area would cover roughly half the size of a tennis court.

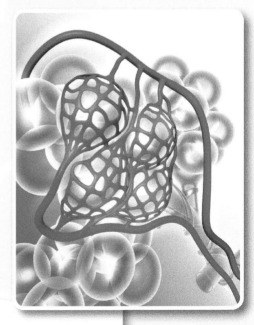

The alveoli are where the oxygen in the air you breathe meets your blood.

Gas Exchange

The alveoli in the lungs have very thin walls, covered with a network of tiny **blood vessels** called **capillaries**. Together, an alveoli wall and a capillary wall are 20 times thinner than a sheet of paper. This means that oxygen can easily cross from the air, through the alveoli walls, and into the blood in the capillaries.

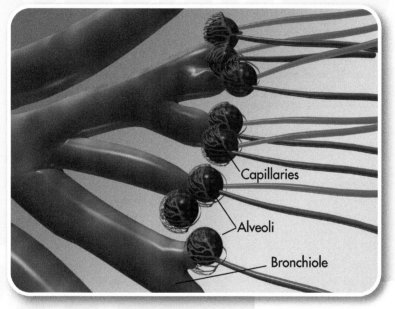

Capillaries

Alveoli

Bronchiole

At the same time, carbon dioxide can pass out of the blood in the capillaries, through the alveoli walls, and be breathed out of the lungs. Carbon dioxide is one of the body's waste products.

Tiny blood vessels called capillaries cover the alveoli in your lungs.

Diffusion

Oxygen and carbon dioxide move in and out of your blood through a process called diffusion. In diffusion, things move from where there is a high concentration (a lot of them) to where there is a low concentration (not a lot of them).

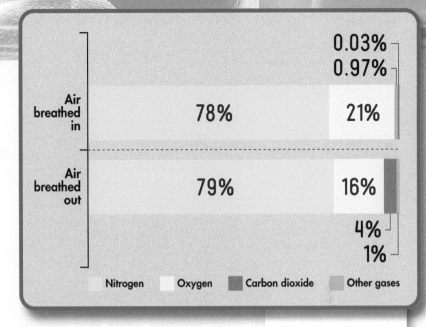

				0.03%
				0.97%
Air breathed in	78%		21%	
Air breathed out	79%		16%	
				4%
				1%

Nitrogen   Oxygen   Carbon dioxide   Other gases

The blood carried to your lungs from other parts of your body has a lower concentration of oxygen than the air you have breathed in, because your body has used up some of the oxygen. So oxygen moves from the air into your blood. At the same time, the blood carried to your lungs has more carbon dioxide than the air, so it moves from your blood and into the air in the lungs.

The air you breathe out has less oxygen and more carbon dioxide than the air you breathe in.

Making a Fizz

You can see diffusion at work when you open a bottle of soda. There is far more carbon dioxide in the drink than in the air outside the bottle—the gas is what makes the bubbles. When you open the bottle, the carbon dioxide in the drink starts to move out of the drink and into the air.

Lung Problems

Healthy lungs allow your body to get all the oxygen it needs. They also allow your body to dispose of carbon dioxide. But sometimes people have illnesses that mean their lungs don't work as well as they should.

Asthma is a common lung condition. It makes breathing difficult. During an asthma attack, the small bronchioles in the lungs get smaller. Their delicate lining can also swell up. This makes them narrower, and so less oxygen can pass through them to the alveoli and the rest of body. The World Health Organization estimates that around 235 million people in world have asthma.

Many people use an **inhaler** to relieve asthma symptoms. The drug goes straight to the lungs, and it relaxes the muscles around the narrow airways.

Number of people with asthma	More than 25 million
Deaths from asthma in 2009	3,388
Number of people per day dying of asthma	9

This chart shows some statistics about asthma in the United States.

New Lungs

Some people with badly damaged lungs are offered transplants. This is when surgeons take healthy lungs from someone who has died and put them inside the person with damaged lungs. Around 1,800 lung transplants are performed every year in the United States.

Germs in the Lungs

Some germs (**viruses** and **bacteria**) do not get trapped by the mucus and hairs in the nose and windpipe. These can get into the lungs and can cause diseases such as bronchitis or tuberculosis. These diseases can affect the amount of oxygen that the lungs can pass into the body.

Tiny particles can also get into the lungs. These can clog up tiny airways, making it difficult for air to pass freely to the alveoli. Some particles can cause a disease called **cancer** to start growing in the lungs.

Vehicle engines send out tiny particles into the air. These can get into the lungs and cause problems.

Stub It Out!

Smoking is one of biggest causes of death and illness in the United States. There are about 443,000 deaths linked to smoking every year. It causes 80–90 percent of lung cancers, and it also causes cancer of the mouth, throat, and voice box. Smoking can also lead to lots of other diseases, such as bronchitis, pneumonia, and emphysema.

The smoke that people draw in kills the tiny cilia hairs in their respiratory systems. This means that mucus can't flow upward and out of the lungs, so dirt and germs are trapped in their lungs. This causes illness and disease.

Peak Flow

How well the lungs work, and their health, can be measured using peak flow equipment. The peak flow is the fastest speed that a person can blow air out of his or her lungs. It is recorded in liters of air per minute.

This line diagram shows the normal peak flow values for different heights of adult men and women.

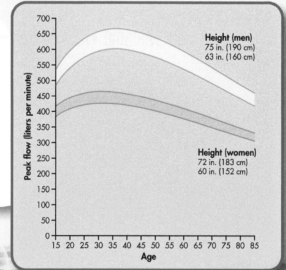

Oxygen Masks

You may have seen people in the hospital with tubes taped to their noses or with breathing masks over their faces. These are delivering higher concentrations of oxygen to them. This is helpful to people who are having breathing problems or heart problems.

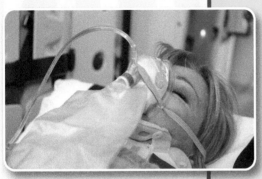

Peak flow is different for men and women, and it also changes with the age of a person and his or her height. People with lung illnesses and diseases—and smokers—usually have lower peak flows than would be expected for their age and height.

Type	% of oxygen
Non-rebreathing face mask	90–100%
Rebreathing face mask	60–90%
Simple face mask	40–60%
Nasal tubes	24–40%
Fresh air	21%

% of oxygen

This bar chart shows how different types of breathing equipment can deliver different concentrations of oxygen to people.

Blood of Life

Your lungs deliver oxygen to your blood, and your blood then carries it to the rest of your body as part of your circulatory system. Your blood makes up around 7–8 percent of your body weight. An average man has 11.8 pints (5.6 liters) of blood, while an average woman has 9.1 pints (4.3 liters) of blood.

Cells and Plasma

Blood is made of lots of different types of cells, including red blood cells and white blood cells. Red blood cells carry the oxygen around your body. White blood cells fight germs that might infect your body.

Blood also contains platelets. These stop you from bleeding to death if you damage your blood vessels. They form clumps, called blood clots, that block the damaged area and stop the bleeding. The liquid that the cells and platelets travel in is called plasma. Around 90 percent of plasma is water, but it also contains certain chemicals.

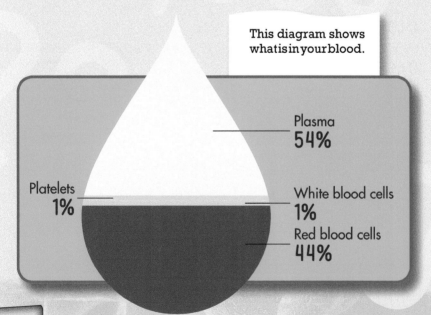

This diagram shows what is in your blood.

Plasma
54%

Platelets
1%

White blood cells
1%

Red blood cells
44%

Making New Blood

Red blood cells, white blood cells, and platelets die and must be replaced. A soft, jellylike substance in the center of your bones does this. This bone marrow makes 100 percent of your red blood cells and platelets. Every second, it generates more than two million red blood cells and about four million platelets.

Bone marrow also makes 60–70 percent of your white blood cells. The rest of your white blood cells are made in some of your body's organs—particular body parts that do special jobs.

A Drop of Blood

Imagine a tiny drop of blood the size of a pinhead. In this drop, there are five million red blood cells, 300,000 platelets, and 10,000 white blood cells. As you can imagine, they are all tiny! A red blood cell is only about 0.0003 inch (0.007 millimeter) in diameter.

Red Blood Cells

Red blood cells are what give blood its color. They pick up oxygen from your lungs and carry it around your body. They are bright red in color when they have collected the oxygen. Once your body has used the oxygen, the red blood cells take waste carbon dioxide to your lungs. These red blood cells are a darker reddish-blue.

Red blood cells live for about 120 days. Then they die and are replaced by new ones from your bone marrow. There are about 25 trillion (25,000,000,000,000) red blood cells in your body!

The flattened disk shape of red blood cells means there is more surface area for the oxygen to cling to.

White Blood Cells

White blood cells help your body to fight infection and diseases. There are three main types, and they can change shape as they get to work! Some totally surround and destroy the germs, while others make chemicals called antibodies that kill or disable the germs. Your body makes a lot more white blood cells when it detects an infection.

Bump up Your White Cells

Getting exercise can nearly double the amount of white blood cells in your body! One cubic millimeter of blood contains 4,500 to 11,000 white blood cells. After exercise, this can go over 20,000. Also, because your blood is pumping around your body faster, they can reach germs more quickly.

Plasma

Plasma carries the red and white blood cells and platelets around your body. It also carries lots of other useful things, including **vitamins**, **minerals**, **hormones**, and waste products. It contains chemicals that help the platelets to clot, and it carries warmth around your body parts.

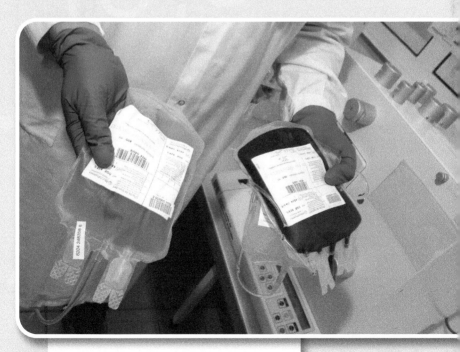

Blood can be separated into its different parts using a machine called a centrifuge. The plasma is the yellowish liquid.

Platelets

Platelets are small fragments of cells. They are only about one-fifth the size of red blood cells. When you damage a blood vessel, such as when you have a cut, platelets gather there. They swell and become sticky. They release chemicals that make substances in plasma turn into sticky threads called fibrin. These form a net, and blood cells get caught in this. A blood clot forms, which dries to become a scab.

It takes three to eight minutes for a small cut to clot and stop bleeding.

Give Blood, Give Life!

Healthy adults can give blood to be used to help sick and injured people. Around 1 pint (470 milliliters) of blood is taken from a **blood donor**. The body usually replaces the white blood cells and platelets within a few days. Replacing all the red blood cells takes a few weeks.

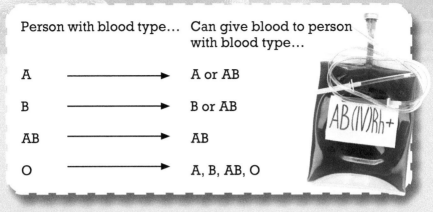

Person with blood type...		Can give blood to person with blood type...
A	⟶	A or AB
B	⟶	B or AB
AB	⟶	AB
O	⟶	A, B, AB, O

Blood Groups

The chemicals in blood can differ slightly. There are four different types of blood, and you have one of these types. The blood types—or groups—are called A, B, AB, and O. It is good to know which blood type you are.

People who need a blood transfusion (blood from someone else put into their body) must have their blood type checked first. Giving people the wrong blood may cause their white blood cells to think the new blood cells are germs and attack them. The new blood could also turn lumpy and make clots.

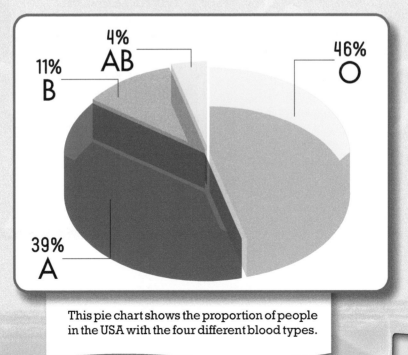

4%
AB

11%
B

46%
O

39%
A

This pie chart shows the proportion of people in the USA with the four different blood types.

Blood Problems

Some people have conditions that affect their blood. Anemia is a common blood condition, and there are lots of different types and causes. With anemia, a person's blood does not have enough red blood cells, or the red blood cells cannot carry enough oxygen. This makes people tired, weak, out of breath, and dizzy. It can cause headaches and can damage the heart, brain, and other organs if it is serious.

Some types of anemia are caused when the red blood cells do not have enough of a chemical called hemoglobin. This is what the oxygen binds onto.

Eating food rich in iron, like kale and nuts such as pine nuts, can increase the levels of hemoglobin in your blood.

	Normal levels of hemoglobin (grams per deciliter)	Anemic level of hemoglobin (grams per deciliter)
Men	13–18	Below 13
Women	12–16	Below 12

DVT

Deep **vein** thrombosis (DVT) is a condition where a blood clot forms in a vein, deep in the body. These can be dangerous if they break away from where they form and travel to places such as the heart, lungs, or brain. If they lodge in these places, they can cause serious damage or even death.

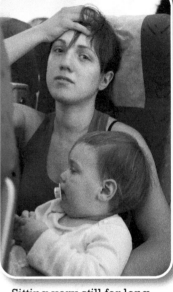

Sickle Cell

Sickle cell anemia is an illness that occurs when the red blood cells develop into the wrong shape. Instead of being round, they are shaped like a crescent. This means they are not as flexible and they can block up blood vessels.

Sitting very still for long periods of time, such as during a long flight, can increase the risk of getting DVT. This is because the blood can slow down and start pooling in the legs, and a clot can form.

No Clotting

Hemophilia is a condition where the blood plasma lacks the chemicals that work with platelets to make blood clots. This means that people can lose a lot of blood after an injury and can also have bleeding inside the body. This can damage organs and can even kill people. Is it usually only men and boys who have hemophilia. Around 1 in 10,000 people are born with this condition.

Transporting Blood

Your blood needs to get to all the parts of your body. It carries the oxygen, energy, and nutrients that your body needs. It picks up oxygen from your lungs and food from your liver. It takes waste products to your lungs and kidneys. Your blood moves around through a huge network of linked blood vessels.

Red Arteries

Most **arteries** carry bright red blood, full of oxygen, away from your heart. They take the blood to your cells. The biggest artery is the aorta. This is the main blood vessel from your heart. It is about 1 inch (2.5 centimeters) in diameter and 16 inches (40 centimeters) long. The blood in your arteries that travels from your heart toward your lungs is reddish-blue. It needs to get back to your lungs for more oxygen.

Vena cava

Aorta

There are about 60,000 miles (100,000 kilometers) of blood vessels in your body.

Awesome Aorta

Your aorta is the biggest artery in your body. But it is tiny compared to a blue whale's aorta. You could crawl though this giant creature's aorta, just like crawling through a playground tunnel!

When you are cold, your brain tells the arteries near your skin to tighten. This stops your blood from getting colder, and you look pale.

Reddish-blue Veins

Most veins carry reddish-blue blood toward your heart. Your body's cells have used the oxygen in this blood. It needs to return to your heart, to then be pumped to your lungs to get more oxygen. The veins going from your lungs back to your heart carry bright red blood, full of oxygen.

The smallest veins are called venules. They join to form bigger veins, which all run into the vena cava—the biggest vein. This is 1.2 inches (3 centimeters) wide and 16 inches (40 centimeters) long.

Branching Arteries

At the end of the aorta, blood starts branching off into smaller arteries. These range from 0.2 inch (5 millimeters) to 0.4 inch (10 millimeters) wide. In turn, these branch into tiny arterioles— only 0.04 inch (1 millimeter) wide.

This pie chart shows where blood is in the body at any one time. There is far more blood in the veins than in the arteries. This is because the blood in the veins is much slower-moving.

Blood travels through the aorta at about 12 inches (30 centimeters) every second.

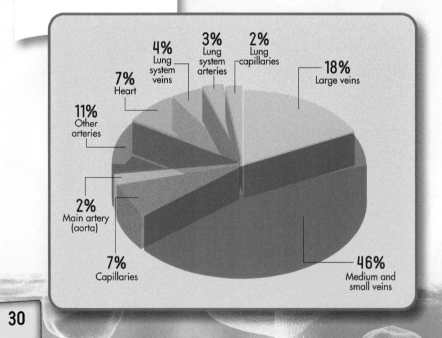

7% Heart

11% Other arteries

4% Lung system veins

3% Lung system arteries

2% Lung capillaries

18% Large veins

2% Main artery (aorta)

7% Capillaries

46% Medium and small veins

Tiny Capillaries

At the end of every arteriole are tiny capillaries. These are really small blood vessels, with walls that are only one cell thick. A human hair is about 100 times thicker than a capillary wall. Blood travels slowly through capillaries, only about 0.02 inch (0.5 millimeter) per second. Most capillaries are about 0.02 inch (0.5 millimeter) long, so blood takes one second to pass through them.

During this one second, oxygen, nutrients from food, and other chemicals move out of the blood. Carbon dioxide and waste chemicals move into the blood from the body tissues around the capillaries. This exchange only happens in capillaries. It does not happen in veins or arteries, because their walls are too thick.

Billions of Capillaries

Capillaries are tiny, but there are billions of them in your body—scientists estimate that there are around 10–40 billion! This means that the total surface area over which these exchanges happen is about 6,460 square feet (600 square meters).

Valves in Veins

The blood in the veins in your legs has to work against the downward pull of gravity to get back to your heart. Your veins have little flaps called valves spaced out along them. Each heartbeat pushes blood through the valves, and these close behind the blood so it can't be pulled back down by gravity.

Problem Blood Vessels

The network of blood vessels spreads throughout every part of your body, to take life-giving oxygen and energy to all your cells and to remove carbon dioxide and other wastes. But some medical conditions can affect blood vessels.

Some people have Raynaud's disease. Small blood vessels in their hands and feet are very sensitive to changes in temperature. Cold temperatures can make them constrict. This interrupts blood flow to their fingers and toes, making them turn white and go numb. It can be painful and can stop people from being able to use their hands properly. There are thought to be about 28 million Raynaud's disease sufferers in the United States.

Raynaud's disease makes the tips of the fingers turn white. Things can go back to normal when they warm up, though.

Bulging Blood Vessels

If a blood vessel wall is weakened, it can bulge out because of the pressure of the blood flowing through it. Sometimes this can be caused by smoking or by high blood pressure. These bulges—called aneurysms—are often in the brain or abdomen (the area below the ribs). They can be very dangerous if they suddenly burst.

Lumpy Legs

When the tiny valves in the leg veins stop working properly, blood can flow backward. This causes blood to collect in the veins, which swell up and get bigger. These varicose veins affect up to three in ten adults. The condition causes achy legs and swollen feet, and makes the veins look like long purple lumps.

People with varicose veins often sit with their legs raised. This helps the blood to flow up the veins and can relieve the aching feeling in the legs.

Pumping It All Around

Your lungs give your blood its oxygen, and your blood vessels deliver the blood to all the parts of your body. Your heart is the vital organ that pumps blood all around your body. It is constantly working to keep you alive, every second, minute, and hour—day and night.

Heart-shaped Heart?

Your heart is about the size of your fist. It is not really heart-shaped at all, it is more like a squishy ball. But it does have two lobes (sections), like the heart shape we think of.

Your heart is located just behind your lower breastbone, which runs down the center of your ribs. Your heart is slightly over to the left side. It is surrounded by your two lungs.

Your left lung is slightly smaller than your right lung, to make room for your heart.

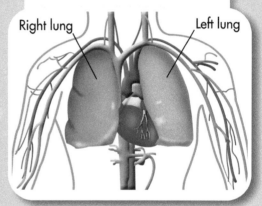

Right lung

Left lung

I ♥ You

We use the heart symbol to show love, and we talk about heartache and heartbreak. Emotions don't actually come from the heart—they come from the brain. But certain emotions can make the heart beat faster, so the heart is used as a symbol for many emotions.

The heart is made of muscle. It is divided into four parts called chambers.

Heavy Heart

A human heart weighs 9–10½ ounces (250–300 grams). Compare this to a blue whale heart, which can weigh 4,000 pounds (1,800 kilograms)—the size of a small car!

Two-sided Heart

There are two sides to the heart, the left and the right. They are separated by a thick wall of muscle called the septum. Each side has an upper chamber, called an **atrium**, and a lower chamber, called a **ventricle**. There is a valve between the atrium and ventricle on each side.

Automatic Pump

A heartbeat is in two parts. First the muscles contract, to squeeze blood out. Then they relax, to let blood in. The contraction happens because of electrical signals sent to the muscles. These signals come from an area in the heart, at the top of the right atrium, called the sinoatrial node.

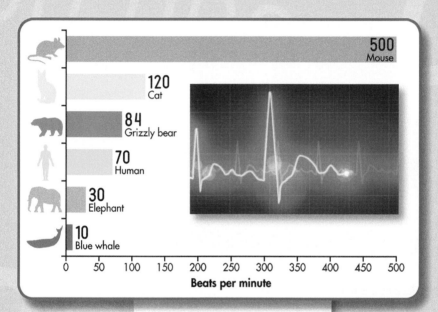

500
Mouse

120
Cat

84
Grizzly bear

70
Human

30
Elephant

10
Blue whale

0   50   100   150   200   250   300   350   400   450   500
Beats per minute

This diagram compares a human's heart rate (the number of beats per minute) with the heart rates of some animals.

Quick!

Adrenaline is a hormone that your body releases when you are frightened or excited. It travels to your heart in your blood. It tells the heart to start beating more quickly, in case you need to get ready for quick action. This is why a sudden scare or nervous situation can make you feel your heart thudding inside you.

Lub-dub, Lub-dub

While you are sitting still, your heart beats around 70 times a minute. Each beat pushes about 2$\frac{1}{2}$ ounces (75 milliliters) of blood from your heart. This means that your heart pumps over 10$\frac{1}{2}$ pints (5 liters) of blood every minute, roughly all the blood in the body.

During exercise, an adult's **heart rate** rises to around 150 beats per minute, with about 6.8 ounces (200 milliliters) of blood pushed out in one beat. This means that about 63 pints (30 liters) of blood are pumped by the heart every minute.

A heart beats:
- over 100,000 times a day
- around 40 million times a year
- over three billion times in an average lifetime.

Hibernation

Some animals, like the mouse below, **hibernate** over cold winter periods. They can go for long periods without eating or drinking. Their body systems slow down so they can conserve energy. Their hearts slow down and they take far fewer breaths. A grizzly bear's heart rate, for example, drops from around 84 beats per minute to around 19 beats per minute during hibernation.

Blood in, Blood out

The valves between the atria and the ventricles only let blood flow one way through the heart. On the left side, blood carrying oxygen comes from your lungs to the atrium. This has small, thin walls. It squeezes weakly to push the blood though the valve and into the ventricle. This has strong, thick walls and can push the blood strongly through another valve and around the rest of your body.

On the right side, blood that has lost its oxygen comes from around your body and into the atrium. The atrium squeezes the blood into the ventricle, which pushes the blood to the lungs, where it can pick up more oxygen.

A doctor can hear the cycle of your heartbeat using a stethoscope.

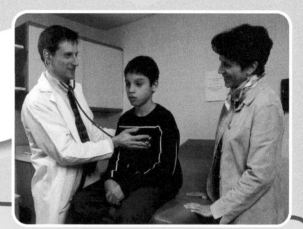

Heart Cycle

The heartbeat that you can hear is the noise made by the valves when they snap shut. The cycle of a heartbeat is:

1. Heart relaxes and atria fill with blood.
2. Atria push blood into ventricles.
3. Ventricles push blood into body and lungs.
4. Heart relaxes again…back to stage 1.

Each cycle takes about four-fifths of a second, when a person is sitting still.

Amount of blood pumped around an adult's body in a day	1,584 gallons (7,200 liters)
Amount of blood pumped around a person's body by the age of 70	40 million gallons (182 million liters)
Distance heart could squirt blood in one beat	30 feet (9 meters)

It takes a lot of blood to keep the body going.

System under Pressure

The blood pumped from the left side of your heart has to reach all your body parts. The blood needs to be under pressure to do this. Imagine if you pinch the end of a hose. You can get the water to shoot farther out of the hose because it comes out at a higher pressure. This is the same for the blood in your body.

A blood pressure measurement has two numbers. One measures the pressure of the blood just after the ventricles contract (called systolic pressure). Another measures the pressure of the blood when the heart relaxes between beats (called diastolic pressure). The units used are mmHg, which stands for millimeters of mercury.

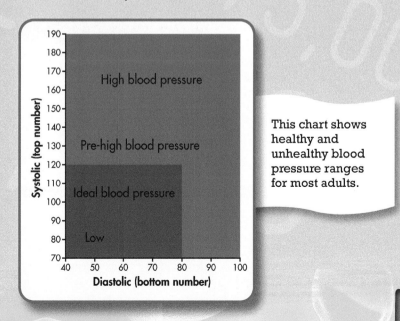

This chart shows healthy and unhealthy blood pressure ranges for most adults.

Problems of the Heart

The heart muscles also need blood to give them oxygen and energy. The heart's blood vessels are called coronary arteries and veins. They run over the surface of the heart and into its muscles.

A heart attack is a common heart problem. It can be caused by a blood clot in a coronary artery. This blocks the blood from going to the heart. If the blood flow to the heart is reduced or stopped, the heart muscles can get damaged and can't contract properly.

Coronary arteries can also get stiff and narrow because of coronary heart disease. This causes pain and makes a heart attack more likely. Around 385,000 people die from coronary heart disease every year in the United States.

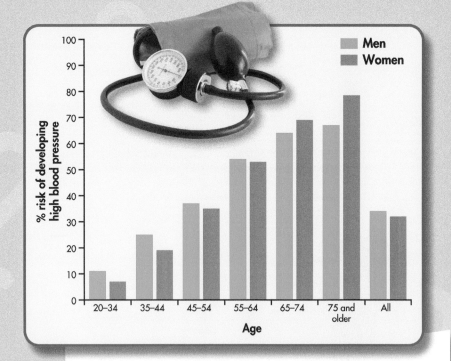

This bar chart shows the risk of developing high blood pressure for certain age groups. It also shows the average risk for any adult. A risk means the number of people likely to be affected. For example, out of 100 men between the ages of 55 and 64, 54 of them will develop high blood pressure.

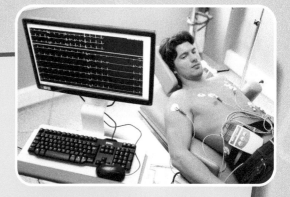

Blocked arteries can cause all sorts of problems in the human body.

Too Much Pressure!

If the blood pressure in the body is too high, this puts a strain on the heart. It makes a heart attack more likely. The problem with high blood pressure is that, often, people don't notice any effects, so they don't know they have it.

Fluttery Heart

Sometimes the electrical messages to the muscles in the heart can make the heart beat quickly, or feel fluttery, or feel like there are extra heartbeats in places. These are called palpitations. They are caused by electrical messages coming from other parts of the heart, or from the normal place but following a different route through the heart muscles. Mostly, palpitations are harmless and the heart will settle back down.

Your Life-Support System

Your heart, lungs, blood, and blood vessels all work together as parts of your respiratory and circulatory systems to keep you alive, every minute of every day. There are countless parts involved, from one heart, to two lungs, to millions of alveoli, to billions of blood cells, to miles of blood vessels. All these parts work automatically without your having to do anything. But you can do some things to keep it all working well.

Take Care of It!

You can help to keep your heart healthy by eating a healthy diet. You need to eat a good balance of protein (to repair cells), carbohydrates (to give you energy), vitamins, minerals, and fats (to carry nutrients around in your blood). Too much fat in your diet can cause problems for your heart and your arteries, while too much salt can cause high blood pressure.

Happy Hearts and Lungs

Apart from eating a good diet, drinking enough water is essential for a healthy body. Getting enough exercise and enough sleep are also important for keeping your heart and lungs healthy.

Age	Maximum salt per day
1–3 years	2 g
4–6 years	3 g
7–10 years	5 g
11 and older	6 g

This table shows the maximum amount of salt that different age groups should eat in one day. People who eat a lot of processed food often eat much more salt than they realize.

No. 1 Killer

Smoking has been identified as causing the most illnesses and deaths in the United States. It causes lung cancer and other lung diseases. It also causes heart disease and high blood pressure. The good news is that people who stop smoking start to get some health benefits right away. Over time, the health benefits get better and better.

Even being happy can keep your heart healthy! Studies have shown that happy people are less likely to develop heart disease than gloomy people.

Test Yourself!

Take a look at the questions below. You will find all the answers somewhere in this book. Check out the pages where the information is if you need reminding of the answers.

1 What special cells in your blood stop you from bleeding to death?
a red blood cells
b white blood cells
c platelets

2 Put these animals in order, starting with the one with the lowest heart rate:
cat; blue whale; mouse; grizzly bear; elephant

3 Air is a mix of lots of gases—which one is it mostly made of?
a nitrogen
b oxygen
c carbon dioxide

4 What is the most common blood type?
a B
b O
c A

5 How much does a human heart weigh?
a 1.8 ounces (50 grams)
b 3¹/₂ ounces (100 grams)
c 9 ounces (250 grams)

6 Which of these blood vessels is around 1.2 inches (3 centimeters) wide?
a vein
b venule
c vena cava

7 During exercise, an adult's heart beats around 150 times per minute and pushes around 6.8 ounces (200 milliliters) of blood out with each beat. How much blood does the heart pump every minute?
a 63 pints (30 liters)
b 85 pints (40 liters)
c 106 pints (50 liters)

8 While sitting quietly at rest, if you take in 1 pint of air with every breath, and you breathe in 16 pints over a minute, how many breaths have you taken in 1 minute?

a 16
b 17
c 18

9 Your blood is made of various amounts of lots of different things. Put these in order, from the largest percentage to the smallest:
white blood cells; plasma; platelets; red blood cells

10 Over an average lifetime of 75 years, how many times will a person's heart beat?

a over 3 million
b over 3 billion
c over 3 trillion

Feel the Pulse!

You can feel your blood pulsing around your body at certain points, called pulse points. These are located at several places on your body. One is in your wrist. Find out where the others are. Then see if you can feel your own pulse. Try counting it to see what your pulse rate (heart rate) is.

Answers:
1c; 2: blue whale (10 bpm), elephant (30 bpm), grizzly bear (84 bpm), cat (120 bpm), mouse (500 bpm); 3a; 4b; 5c; 6c; 7a; 8a; 9: plasma (54%), red blood cells (44%), white blood cells and platelets (each 1%); 10b

Glossary

alveoli tiny air sacs in your lungs where oxygen and carbon dioxide are exchanged

artery blood vessel that carries blood full of oxygen away from your heart and around your body

asthma lung disease that causes the airways to contract, making it hard to breathe

atrium (plural: atria) upper chamber of the heart

bacteria tiny living things found almost everywhere, including inside and outside your body

blood donor someone who gives some of his or her blood so it can later be used to help people who have lost blood in an accident or through illness

blood vessel any of the tubes in the body that blood flows through

bronchiole smallest, thinnest air tube in the lungs

bronchus (plural: bronchi) one of the two main branches of the windpipe that goes into the lungs

cancer disease that causes certain cells in the body to grow abnormally; there are lots of different types of cancer, depending on which cells are affected

capillary smallest blood vessel in the body

cell tiny unit that makes up all parts of your body; different body parts are made of different kinds of cells

germ any tiny living thing that can cause disease

glucose type of sugar found in the blood; glucose gives you energy

heart rate speed at which your heart beats, measured in beats per minute

hibernate be in a sleeplike state, where the body processes such as the heartbeat slow down

hormone substance that helps control cells and helps organs perform tasks

inhaler device that allows medicine to get straight into the lungs, by breathing it in

mineral substance formed in the Earth's crust

nerve cell special cell responsible for sending messages around the body

organ part of your body that performs a particular task, such as the heart or lungs

oxygen gas that humans and other animals need in order to stay alive

respiratory system bodily system related to breathing, involving the exchange of oxygen and carbon dioxide

vein blood vessel that carries blood toward your heart, so it can receive oxygen

ventricle lower chamber of the heart

virus tiny living thing that can enter your body and cause illness and disease

vitamin substance that people need in order to grow properly

Find Out More

BOOKS

Ballard, Carol. *Heart and Blood* (Body Focus). Chicago: Heinemann Library, 2010.

Seuling, Barbara. *Your Skin Weighs More Than Your Brain and Other Freaky Facts About Your Skin, Skeleton, and Other Body Parts* (Freaky Facts). Mankato, Minn.: Capstone, 2008.

Taylor-Butler, Christine. *The Circulatory System* (True Book). New York: Scholastic, 2008.

Taylor-Butler, Christine. *The Respiratory System* (True Book). New York: Scholastic, 2008.

Walker, Richard. *Human Body* (Eyewitness). New York: Dorling Kindersley, 2012.

WEB SITES

anatomyarcade.com/games/gamesCirculatory.html
Test your knowledge with crossword puzzles and word searches!

kidshealth.org/kid/htbw/heart.html
Here you can find out lots of information about the circulatory system, and there are diagrams to click on and find out more.

www.neok12.com/Circulatory-System.htm
On this web site there are some fun games to test your knowledge of the circulatory system.

FURTHER RESEARCH

You could visit your local library to see if there are any books on the respiratory and circulatory systems. You could also do some research of your own. Figure out your pulse and breathing rates while you are at rest and after you have been exercising.

Index